Praise for

Inside Violence
Violence Inside

These are crushing, quiet, deeply introspective poems in which language cannot be pinned down and death and life, boredom and dread, senselessness and love exchange places so often it becomes undeniable they share an identity within us all. Lovely Raju's poetry defies scrutiny, and in that disarming ambiguity, dissolves distinctions between the other and the self.

—Michael J. Deluca
author of *The Jaguar Mask*

Pulsing with vulnerability and openness, these verses respond like new scars to the violence that wounds them into existence. Lovely Raju runs on a surrealist nerve that is not any kind of flight: the book's haunting slippages and shape-shifting figures assemble a "woven love" tough enough to bear all the ways we shred and tear. These poems—haunting and healing--"borrow the sky."

—Matthew Kilbane,
author of *The Lyre Book: Modern Poetica Media*

At once an extremely American book - about the way violence enters us, circulates between us - and a wholly unique book. The speaker observes the world with the clarity of a stranger, the precision of the language creating a peculiar intensity.

—**Johannes Göransson**,
author of *Summer*

Inside
Violence
Violence
Inside

FLOWERSONG
PRESS

poetry by
LOVELY RAJU

FLOWERSONG
PRESS

FlowerSong Press
Copyright © 2025 by Lovely Raju
ISBN: 978-1-963245-10-3

Published by FlowerSong Press
in the United States of America.
www.flowersongpress.com

Book Cover Design by Edward Vidaurre

Set in Adobe Garamond Pro

NOTICE: SCHOOLS AND BUSINESSES
FlowerSong Press offers copies of this book at quantity discount with
bulk purchase for educational, business, or sales promotional use. For
information, please email the Publisher at info@flowersongpress.com.

To Lovely, my mother—the first poem I ever knew

Note from the Author:

The shooting at Robb Elementary School greatly inspired me to write this manuscript. These poems not only talk about gun violence but also domestic and climate violence. This is likely a study or remedial study of violence that seeks resolution for existing trauma or justice for a half-dead mother, and/or is exhausted by experiencing different forms of violence. I hope these poems strike a nerve.

table of contents

I. Inside

II. Violence

III. Violence

IV. Inside

**Inside
Violence
Violence
Inside**

I.

Inside

Violence

The balcony is as calm
as still water.
The violence remains inside
This calmness.
The car right before me
Watching my every move.
When I look into its eyes,
It turns into a scary spook.
A man carrying a rifle seems
to be going haunting.
I do not know
What/who will he haunt?
He aims at a deer to kill it.
Violence is in his eyes.
Violence is in his body.
The eyes of a woman
Killed my reality.
How sweet the violence!
The car still remains spooky
Even in my fancy when
She borrows the sky for me.

Anger issue

Sometimes you look like
the fear that wakes me up

at night. When you cook,
Is that fire in your face?

I might be daydreaming
though that is not impertinent.

When you broke the glass
of water and hit my back,

You weren't you, you were
red furnace under the pan,

I was like vegetables,
simmered. Minutes later

You were you. And you
Poured cold water on me.

The other day you planted
an oak tree, you looked like

a shovel that didn't mercy the soil.
You took me to a psychiatrist.

It didn't make any sense.
Did you not ever see you

when you turned into fire?
It burns not because of nightmares.

If you are a sun you think
for me. Let me tell you one thing.

I don't deserve it.

Shadow

A person follows the vulnerability
of a fear driven body.
I notice perhaps it is a shadow
that I do not possess.
It races the vine of blood to
keep me away from sanity.

My shadow does not hurt me.
My shadow is not lengthy.
My shadow does not have dark teeth.

It is someone else's from the silence.
The silence that I created in the air.
The silence that makes them kill
the memories I frame.

I could roar like the current of water.
I could tear the sky with sound waves.
I just wanted birds to sing me a song
and flowers to make me fall in love.

The grimacing shadow does not seem
to listen to the words I speak now.
Maybe I would sing a lullaby for
the serene tulips, loving birds
and for the flying pollen.

Then I would roar not to scare
the host of stars but to
drive the shadows away.
I would still invite them to
my home when they become humans.

Theory of color

If color gives birth to hate,
Then what is the color of hate?
The water like an insane athlete
(That knows not where to go)
took two boys the other day.
The water had a color that
No one could name, no one
Could measure its wavelength.
It only wanted to eat something.

My mother says the tone of my skin
Changing with time. In summer
The heaven drips more light
On my body, people say I look
Beautiful but when I look at my
Skin I find I am getting uglier.
When I change color, the only person
I hate is me, the change for acceptance.
Again, what is the color of my hate?
The bees hate to leave the tulips,
Still they go back home
No matter how unsafe the air is.
It killed me several times and again
I keep changing my color.
My hate for me is so humane.

Die and feel safe

I walk along the hilly road,
Smell the summer, dissolve
Myself into the mirth.
Still something in my mind.
I do not know its origin.
While kissing the aroma of the air
I ask, what is the possibility of falling
A star on my head.
I do not know when was the last time
A meteor hit the earth.
Is it coming towards me?
I do not know how violent the floating
Object could be.
This violence is acceptable.
What is the possibility of displacement of
A planet from its orbit that feeds me?
If that happens now, that is acceptable.
What is not acceptable is a mad bullet
That is directed to my body.
There are Thousands of them.
How do I slow their velocities to just
Let them kiss me softly.
Does the air help me?
Or has it already been a victim!
Maybe be back where you were.
Be soil to feed the burnt plants.
Maybe die today and feel safe.

God's violence

I want the flow,
A flow of God's violence,
More and more,
Then little away of the torn
Light, a light that my hair
spews will dry the sun,
Yet I will see me burn and
again move on saving
the earthly stains that
were given to my body.

Fear

I heard people say silence
gives birth to something new.
When I am sitting at the
bus stop all alone, the silence from
my back scares my nerves.
The other day, silence spoke to me.
I was leaning against the wall
That had no complaint,
To give birth to a newer self.
A bullet broke the glass of windows
in order to join me.

A meditation on the cosmos,
A leather body, vitality of the
words ceasing the motion again.
When I get on the bus, two people
talk about politics, after minutes
They argue and get violent.
I expect to hear the sound of a bullet.
Bus stops, I get down, they get
more violent. I rush to my room.

Repentance

Your story now daunts me,
Now and then, day and night.
Someone walks behind me
the person walks parallel.
Whenever I turn back or turn
Aside, nothing stays.
Only the empty apartment or
the spreading field of maize.
I know it is not you or your
shadow that wants revenge.
You are a person who
Just simply avoids the bee
That bites without a reason.
Because you didn't even learn to
pluck a flower from the garden.
It is not you, it is your story
That I made and hid in my sleeve.
Story lies in my bed.
Story eats my blood.
An old man the other night
Came into the room said
"There is still time, there is still
Ways to get a good sleep"
I heard he was my grandfather.

Bereavement

An unknown sapling
in my yard.
It carried an offspring
in its bud,
A babyflower, eyes closed.
It reminded me of a fourteen
year old girl who grew
my sibling in her womb.
It was like my mother.
It was my mother.
And what was growing
on its stem was my sibling.
I fenced them well.
Fed them every day,
prayed to God for them.
One day a storm killed
my mother and sibling
while God was sleeping.

Environmental safety

You sit there in peace.
I see if anything is coming,
towards you, at a fast pace
like a comet (it could be a tiny
man made comet) to lie you
down by force forever.

I stand before you, unknown
of who is behind or above me
trying to throw pebbles. But
you talk, go on with your
beautiful banter. Smile
and kill me in this way.
I will not kill the fly
that disrupts

the flow of your lips.
I would say please go away.
You are safe from curses
into the air someone poured.
I have already eaten them.
You sit there, smile and
kill me in that way.
I will hold the bullet with
my hand to dye your lips.

I feel

I feel a flower in my eyes.
Then a garden blossoms with
a sky lost in the petals.
I feel another home grows,
without the man who sold
his blood for shelter.
He is lying on the platform.
I feel he is still living.
A stray cat calls my name.
His eyes are full of sandwiches
that I hold in my hand.
I feel the sandwiches
in his belly making nutrients
for my cornea. I tell him
not to vomit the love.
He rushes to the bush.
I don't know why.
I feel another corpse in my
eyes, a feast for flies.
all the petals in the garden
turn into bullets.
I feel the sky is already dead.

Driving an evil away

I take out what I can
from this hole.
The darkness of a soul,
A road forgotten for
the excess crowd,
excess water on a planet.
It can move without
an exit plan.
Its mobility independent of
the wound of its surface.
I walk on it and take out
what I can from the complexity
of its existence.
It seeks a resolution for its body,
goes in the wrong direction.
Water flows over the tree.
Heat touches the balcony.
Boiled rice for robins
becomes dried rice again.
I take out what I can
from this hole. I take out my demon.
A mountain eats up excess water.

If there was

If there was anything else
you would want me about you.

I hope you never feel like a
squirrel inside the sun darkening

the ocean with its fake light.
You doubt, double fear, manifold

the scarcity of a craven earth.
You hide the woven love of a man if

the others see it and loot it
from the heart of fragility.

I know man needs freedom.
Maybe he will agree to face the violence.

He will adorn the world as you
dreamed, like a child in its mother's chest.

You show love today, it's time,
to the sunlight, to brighter waters of the ocean.

If the violence is your neighbor,
treat it well, someday you will play with violence.

She

She, far from
the melting point.
She, the woman now and
no longer stenchy like
nightmares.
While she walks alone,
I know she is not looking
for any violence but she's
looking at it with awe.
The sun still working
on healing a non tactile
bodily hole.
When I ask her out,
She says she is scared of
violence, the violence
that leaves no damage
on organic structure.

Lost Gem

She wonders
if violence ever regrets.
A mother waiting
for her kids, asks,
Does violence cry?
(they never come back)
Violence loses emotion.
A stormy day finally wins.

Danger

Danger is around the summer
Danger in the sunlight, a bullet.
Danger that might kill you.
Danger that is a nightmare.
My kids are afraid to go out.
Because danger has become infectious.
And sorrowfully this is how
the summer is propagated to
Be violent among the angels.
The door of heaven is closed.
They play in the room with their parents
Or watch the adventurous cartoons
And garner courage to face the gun.
The Gods are still confused about what to do.

Insecurity

If no other things paused
The motion of my legs today
Like love for myself, the desire
To live in the world a little
While though with all painful
uncertainties, I would walk
Into the clouds and strangle
The thunderstorms that scare
The roses in the garden, or
I would stand by them with a
big canopy and save the petals.
Now I only watch them shiver
And feel how insecure they are
Like kids who couldn't beat bullets.
Maybe the roses will not die today.
I will be there to relieve their trauma
And say, not too bad, you are alive,
A bit insecure but you are lucky, you
Will never have to worry about guns.

II.

Violence

What is Violence?

Trying to kill my god is a violence.

Domestic violence

Perhaps love is forced out of
home where now a cry stays,
Sprawls whose imaginary legs
soon would kick the skyline.
The person still seems arrogant,
his drunk eyes want more chaos.
A cry is the sweet music that
he wants for a sound sleep?
What if that legs tear the horizon,
What if the ocean becomes empty
And all water returns to heaven.
Still you want havoc that leads
To the end of the world?
You would prefer to love, to get
showered in the rain I guess.

Domestic violence 2

Today you talk to me
in a different way.
You talk in violence.
Your hand acts like a weapon.
You throw all the kitchen
utensils on the floor,
a photo frame of us as well.
Mechanical noise fills the room.
The walls cannot take it anymore.
Your face turns into a red giant,
The face that makes me scared.
You leave after you mess things up.
Your eyes do not see me bleed.

Absence

you don't know
what you killed.
you didn't even tell me
you wanted to hurt.
like a bird through sunlight
I wanted to fly.
my body was not made of pain.
did you not know before?
you walked away from
the door of my heart.
we could venture out
together to see the sky.

I wash the messed up kitchen.
alone. jeans on the floor.
I expect them to carry a letter
that says 'Sorry'.
It carries my blood instead.

A woman in Hijab

A woman in Hijab at the park
talks with another woman
who literally wears nothing.
I pretend to see two flowers
but I see nothing but two
flowers emitting the aroma
       of a morning sun.

I pretend to hear the sound
of the aroma but I hear nothing
but two moons lying on earth.
what I am actually doing
       They do not realize.

I sketch eternity
for flowers on the bench.
Some people with weird looks pass.
They have the liberty to pass by.
I have the liberty to sketch,
with or without a pencil.

They have freedom to wear
whatever petals they want.
And numbers, density,
thickness of it might vary
depending on one's propensity.

A flower full of petals reminds me
of my home. I see my sister
and my mother and a woman
who never talked to me but cared.

I killed my son

I place my ear to the wall
to learn if the bricks speak.
A tremor temporarily deafens
me that originally comes from
my body. He lives inside
the flesh. When the night
gallops the noise of the suburb,
Sometimes I hear him sing
and ask a lot of questions.
What makes you look sad?
How difficult is life? Is it safe
to walk along that avenue? Etc.
The other day he insisted
that I bring him to earth.
I burnt my flesh and killed him.

Alike

The person sitting on the bench
looks at me differently.
He seems suspicious.
Maybe I too am a danger to him.
But I walk nicely and smile by myself.
I picture his frown as a weapon
that took the life of a bird.
I wear a decent outfit.
My hair is a bit long but combed.
What is different between us?
The color of the shirt?
We should be the same
under the same sky.
The cloud at any time
would act like a hose.
We will be different if
The rain only splashes you.
Momentarily the clouds shower both of us.

Anti-funeral

Beside your right thought
you could possibly have
left the idea of your left
shoulder that never
bears your weight now.

You were right,
We were not right.
We pushed the boundaries
Of the spheres that are no
longer spherical.

You left a left hand
written letter that used
our blood as ink.
Our veins shrunk
like the phenomenon
of empty balloons.

You were right,
We were not right.
We were a stack of papers
dumped into the water.

A deer

A deer eats leaves beside the window.
I stand, watch him through the glass.

The air conditioner stops shouting now
I realize why, I do not realize its mind

As it runs and throws away my mood.
I find no aesthetic in its loud cry.

The night still keeps me awake to
paint my face with brown dim light

That comes from a leaf in his mouth.
He sees me see him but he is not afraid,

He looks into my eyes, licks the glass,
Perhaps becomes sympathetic thinking

I am in the zoo and he is free to roam.
I realize this deer is so humane unlike the others.

Summer song

Two birds on the bough.
Two people on the balcony.
They kiss each other while
I kiss the warm lips of summer
With an artificially built heart.
the sun glued shattered pieces.
Its light holds them together

For me to breathe another morning.
Sometimes lovers can be violent
Physically or mentally. Stains on
Body might go away soon but
The ones that get inside are
permanent, sticky. I rubbed
some of my memories with
the meteor rock and the rock
got damaged heavily. I look at
The birds again, feel ecstatic to
See them making nice memories.
I hope none of them turns a load.
The birds fly, two people go back
To their room. I fall in love with the
summer, a potential non-violent lover.

Unknown

The other time it rained like regular tears.
What people call the limit of our visibility
now comes to touch my guts of pain.
I have a backache either to carry

the shapes of your numerous faces
and bones that no longer follow the
principles of calcification yet hole to
unmask the frame of infinity through

the door still left unhinged in the desert
It rains people. It rains their memories u nlike
the tears of a man whose hair dissolves
into the sands of water that they call their h ome

Black retina, an apple sugar, an umbrella
an amphibious cloud cloudy. Above your
Head a mountain with moon flies with no
flues for the wound stored for years now

Bullet proof skin

I want to be a tree
Immediately, I wonder
If the sun could help.
Or if again I am born
On this planet,
If again I exist
as a living being,
I would be a tree.
So that I could survive
one or two or more bullets.

Anatomy of violence

I have to go back to the house
and get some stuff done before
The mystery of human psychology
unfolds. We would only saw
Your head to see what happens
There just before people mourn
For the unexpected death of their
Friends, family and relatives.
What happens when you see a blind
Walk, the pious talk to their God.
What happens when people win.
We will see if we can set a neutral
Preference for the wavelength of light
That your eyes receive from others.
Devils have been there for years?
You want to get rid of them, no worries.
We will do a bonfire on your head and
Eat barbecued devils to make you a human.

Betrayal

I want to count how many
bones of my mental health
are broken after you fall onto
me like a roller coaster:
a chance to drive into
the vast possibility of pain.
the nearest star turning into a moon,
a lamp for a dark room is absurd.
I came home with vegetables,
watered your favorite tulip
in the garden that was thirsty.
You were on the bed with
A woman, naked. For instance,
I thought that was me.
I watered the petals of tulips again
And turned into water.
Does water have bones?
I might have forgotten the math
I learned at school.

Exile

This is not too deep.
It would not be hard to
make it by myself.
I do not call anyone even
Not a goat roaming around
For healthy grass beside the trap.
A corpse is trying to get up.
Am I the corpse? If not
Why am I here in the grave?
Someone dug it for me.
I thought it was heaven.
I climb up after years
You come on the shore
Say nothing fill the grave,
A shovel still in your hand.
A man smoking cigarettes yells
At you. I say I am not scared.
You keep silent and leave.
The man asks me to live like the sky.

Healing

I wanted security from the sky.
Violence of storm kills
seedlings, Shake my home,
Frightens me in the night.
I wanted security from the sky
While I could not secure myself
From things that I do every day.
That burns my heart that kills me
Slowly. Without a reason you sit on
the couch, ask not to blame anyone.
Scratches all over my body.
You kiss them and cut my big nails.
A heart full of nicotine, you tear open my
Left chest, get them out.
It beats better than before.
Again the violence of the storm comes.
This time the seedlings remain alive.
You, as the form of air spread to my blood.

Insecurity 2

There is an indication of adversity
In the bone of the street, invisible.
Only the person sees it knows
Not how to assuage the accident
That never was an accident,
Rather a conspiracy against
The simplicity of a soul.
I walk now slowly as
No other route was created.
You might come from behind
From the left or right of the blue
lane, you might fall from the sky.
I wander with a deep breath in my tongue
When the light is red, I pause to see
If I am alive for the next step.
I come home, still smell of
you around the air. I come
Home leaving the street
Alone with crowds and
Possibility of damage.
Sorry, I couldn't
Resist myself from being selfish.

Eviction

There was no building here.
No hanging lamp
No concrete clothed road.
There was little grove
Where raccoons breastfed
Their offspring.
There was a bush in here
Inside that the fireflies lived
With their family.
They ate all the light of stars
for you when they heard you
wanted to move in the shrub.
Later you showed your real face
And made the fireflies homeless.

Insanity

Where you meet these strange ideas
The brown hair did you soak into
Exudes of the insanity of the sky?
The sky that creeps on your head
Like an animal that an astronomer
Saw in space, maybe in a dream,
He drank a little of the light that
Someone liquified, what a discovery.
People would call him mad because
He acted like the animal that was seen
In space that had eaten the little crust
Of the sun before the sun was in its
Mother's womb in a shape of a man
That was exactly like your ugly nose.
That mad man was born on the day
When you as nutrients were roaming
Around his mother's stomach and you,
You were born after your father had eaten
An apple before making love with your mother.
He was inside the apple in a different form.
Ideas you make, could liquefy people's pain
And violence. I will drink them. Go insane.

Savior

I bought a jar of love.
The jar was made of hatred.
Hatred was made of their touch.
Someone kissed the earth's plates.
I was one of the plates.
The ocean fell on my body
But it could not break the bones and
the fire of it wanted to embrace the sky
To burn a moon. You came out of
nothingness to eat the flame of
hate from their hearts.
You saved the earth.

Flood the desert

Next time you look at the frame,
make sure you hold the water onto your palm.
the one will scour relation to your gene.
You hold the protein on your tongue
in case an apocalypse appears without
the intervention of God.
Either an animal that walks without blood,
or an animal that smells the sweat moves
away splintering the wholesome of the flesh.
Irony you don't see it in his mouth.
It is there and yours is a decoy
decaying the balance of atmospheric health.
Part of the ecology of body ruins again.

Angels in the park

When I pass this
neighborhood
to go to work,
angels from god
play in the park.
I slow down
on the sidewalk or stop
pedaling the bike
to see them swing
in the air.
They ride horses
that never run.
They ride fishes
that never swim.
When angels waved me
back the other day.
I did not go to work.
I played with them and
vowed to make a planet
that does not burn their wings.

Climate Injustice

1
(The Cyclone)

An owl cries for her baby.
Dead body is found nowhere.
The storm again is a good
Killer of unborn dreams.

My father mourns for the tree.
The trunk lies on the ground,
Sleeps and soon will die.

He planted it years ago.

2
(The Wildfire)

Heaven now turns hell.
Wildfire burns the feathers
Of the parrot, now she crawls,
Crawls to breathe a little more,

Fire growls behind the tail.
Death waves before fatigued eyes,
Yet she hopes to live again.

3
(The Drought)

Sun is trying to burn
The scalps of my parents
In the paddy land.
They wonder if the sweat
Acted like the water.

A little white cloud turns
Into a canopy over their
Shoulders, but mother wants it
To be fierce and to pour in the land as rain.

4
(The Poverty)

Salt water strangles the crops,
Makes us starve and my
Old granny will die
Soon of hunger.

III.
Violence

What is violence?

To a moonlit starry night
Electric eyes are violence

Ode to violence

Violence is in animals' tongues.
Violence is in hatred.
Violence is in love.
When I am spiritually
Violent, God gets severely hurt.

Violence is all animals' built-in feature. Making it emotionally
and physically safe or minimal makes us humans.

Another world

I walk toward the ocean
        to sail a boat.
You can lie there on sand
    and talk to the seagull.
    Do not hold my leg.
Entice the waves by your
            Fake body
Or shake a vein of air.
The sky is already naked
    and so are the beach and water.
    You wear a makeup on your skin
        to coat the wounds.
    Someone is still behind you
            hungry for your flesh.
    See their behemoth teeth.
I have nothing to fight the demon
    that already ate up the city.
Walk with me to kiss the horizon.
    We will find a habitable land.

Addictive

I still find no difference in
how he weaves his pain.
We go on saying, stop.
Enough of violence with
your body. Maybe clean
The dust on the mirror.
You should look at yourself,
Maybe ask why the cells wrinkle.
We see the rainbow,
He sees the smoke of cigarettes.
We say the summer sun is sweet.
He says, that is the fireball.
When it rains, he prays
a shower of alcohol.
He treats his body savagely
Like it is not his own. Someone
mistakenly put him in there
And he soon wants to escape it.

Exile 2

He lies there like an object
that never displaces its standing
without any external force.
People never stumble to say
that he is my father.
I knit my existing guts of pain,
and hell no, I will have to
end it first to get another job
of the same kind.
They celebrate instead of crying.
Wife of the lying person
does not look sad. She is
compassionately strong or she has
no room for new grief.
My father later comes and unveils
the clothing from that person's
face. He says he does not look
like me, I am not dead.
People bury the lying person and
throw my father out of the space.
I still knit existing guts of pain.
My mother still remains a silent strong woman.

Healing 2

I know how to make
a sad song, how to
croon how to wash my body
Inside which people put hate.
I have nightmares, I talk to them.
Want my blood? Take and go away.
It has been years,
I have seen all their faces.
Yet I go about with fear in
my sleeve. I shower for hours
with hot water, simmer my skin
And let it grow again from the beginning.

The origin

When I was in the star,
I had no eyes, no hair.
I didn't speak to the
moon as it had no ears
and I had no tongue.
We grew inside her
stomach as crystal balls
and sprang for years.
She vomited us when
We were more than chaos.
Then we appeared as planets.
Later we got eyes to see
our home in the sky.
we got tongues to tell her
"take us back to your lap."
Then we got guns for violence.

The life of a star

1

We waited for the light.
We waited to hit our eyes.
We saw how we were
growing partially
wrapped in darkness.

2

Before she ran out
of fuel (billions of years later),
she grew, sheltered
and served billions of other lives.
This is an answer to the
question why a star has to live so long.

3

Life is an ordered combination
of elements.
Whether you are
alive (conscious) or not.
It does not matter to the universe.
In fact, something
that produces light has a life.

God's pronoun

The ocean envies me
when the storm in my heart
rises and turns fatal.
You wouldn't notice a single
hair in my chest move.
When gravity works for me
most, I spread sand in the air
to become one of their particles.
When people crowd around me,
I sit alone away and don't speak
about my silent god with them.
I don't know god's pronouns.

In the theater

I tried to cry in the theater
After watching a movie.
The protagonist was killed.
Still she was in his arms.
She drank the venom and
Chose to not leave him.
That was a world where
The villain was the protagonist.
After weeping for almost an hour
my friend asked me what I was made of?
Listen, the cloud stole all my tears.
When they leave me behind,
When a meteor falls on me,
I save my sorrow inside my hair.
When it rains I cry with the sky.

Anatomy of hate

H ate all the other letters.
He was hungry.
We can't write anything now.

People need food.
Give him food.
Food for stomach,
Food for heart and soul.
If H you think it is a problem
And you want to get rid of it,
Cook food for yourself,
Eat and feed people you hate.
They have been hungry as well.

IV.

Inside

Empty or full does not matter
Matters the degree of tolerance

The dream of memoir

I lie somewhere, maybe the bed is translucent.
Below the insane current of water. The water on
Fire, fire on water, a silent river feeding the ocean
apparently. Feeding its mother. Another sky
dawning through my eyes. I wake up to fly to
my home. I fly like I swim in the water.
My hands are the moving paddles. Legs
accelerate my speed. I do not believe in
my motion. I make sure I am not damn dreaming.
A car evolves tarry smoke and burns my wings. I fall
down to the earth. Mother is washing my dirty shirts in
the bathroom alone and singing. I go there and lend a hand.

Time travel 2

Through the mirage
We saw an ocean of sun.
A photon of light was lost there.
It wanted to fall onto our roof.
Someone way more
powerful than a soft voice.
shovels in their hands
silenced the sky.
We escaped to escape the light.
A drop of it we could take.
Our homes were homes
Of termites.
We settled on an old earth
and began to understand
the petroglyph of our ancestors.

Let it come

It is not going to
make the sky fall
in astonishment.
doves will not stop
by the song
we will be singing.
Flowers have not bloomed
to smell their aroma.
It might not be as pure
as the heart of a man
who bleeds for others.
Maybe we will consider
soaking it into his vein.
We will see how it is
shaped this time to
Shape us.

Climate crisis

Father drives a shabby
truck on a muddy road
when the fuel crisis is
everywhere.
A sapling standing
alone before him stops
his journey.
He makes a home
there where we grow
old with a dying planet.

Climate Crisis in My (Un)known Dream

(1)

A giant human shadow on earth
Engulfs the ocean and cloud
Remains arid now heavy hearted
Angel there praying for light.

Mother sitting in the sun.
In the kitchen she cooks something
She stands still, tap is on
Basin is clogged, water soon
Floods our planet.

Star dust around her face,
My son playing in the backyard
Fears the shadow, I say
It is your granny, look.

Mother comes down now sits
In the air right beside my boy.
In the kitchen she moves and
Cries, no sound, I see her chop
A big onion, and no one is there
Outside my son and mother.

(2)

A coffin
We were only two
The main door was closed.

Indoor that goes to other room
Stood alone,
No path, before us, a wall
We saw everything through.

The earth was shaking now from inside
Soon maybe, soon wave would explode,

The disaster, the homeless people
Wandering under the sky

The earth looked dull,
The climate was so indomitable.

Someone said, stay, you are safe there.

Mask

I ask her to name the fear.
Aliens reside inside humans.
There is a mask on everything.
That surface might not look ugly.
That might be scary for our eyes.
Who is not ready for the shock?
What is it the sky wears?
The ocean is never found naked.
I ask her to take off the mask.
She begins to skin herself.
I still love the way she is.

Question

I do not play with my mother
anymore but I still watch me
play with her. Besides, I watch
how people play with me now.
I remember you asked me about
the silence. I buried my words to
listen to a song of love. The play
does not have any rhythm but it has an
uneven tone, pitifully. I wrote a
lyric in the hope that someone
would come and sing. Someone
came, fortunately, but walked
away with it and never sang for
me. You asked me about my
vigor. It is in the sound of rain.

Heavy substance

A dragonfly on the head of a deer.
Something they gave me weighs a lot.
I do not name it as it is cliché.
If I reveal, it is still phony to them.
The story means nothing to a cloud
That is already forced to look down, to
Start a journey immediately upon summon.
Cloud and me like the deer shake
Heavily to get lighter to the gravity.
They like the dragonfly, tactile decoy,
Non displaced relative to our dimension.
No matter what beauty the sky holds
You look at your shoulder and balance.
I mow the lawn down here so mildly that
the grasses know nothing about it, and I await
reconciliation of two heavy weighted existences.

Return

While in the crowd
if you find yourself lost,
head to the avenue of dust.
In a mild distance,
sitting a person with
a dead soul.
You know who is
holding the sky,
or the complex geometric
error of the heart,
and how a body bends
with time and space.
That is you or me,
or me without your touch.
A biological feeling ends
when you put a stain of love
elsewhere, and there everything
is done with the discourse
that fails to be appeasing.
Just call my name with your lips.
The city is not yet heartless.

In between

She stands alone against my
spinal cord with a dagger in
one hand and a tulip in the other.
In her mouth she produces
venom to swallow the exude.
Thorns in her stomach gradually
melts without the excess heat
of the sun. I water the flower,
and ask the owner of the sky
to give it a new life. Maybe the soul
of a pained man. I put sand
on my tongue to sharpen
the dagger and I act like
a jellyfish. Now she moves.
A person is going to die to live.

Adaptation

A sunglass covers her eyes.
Some people always love to
hide the pain behind a curtain
of varied colors. Some of them
are made of light and some are
of light membranes of the body.
She goes and never comes back.
A little bird already learned a
lesson when it falls from the nest.
It has already mastered how to balance.
I never blame the mother squirrel
for leaving the kitty. The sky is still
alone although she has held billions
of stars in her chest. There will be
a time when you fly like a bird.

The Woodman

He walks along the horizon.
The willow shakes in joy.
He laughs like a violent cloud.
The light hasn't seen his dirty teeth.
People run away from him.
People fear his unlike shirt.
People see violence in his beard.
They say he is a noxious evil.
But he is not dangerous at all.
He feels someone in the air.
Yesterday night he talked for a
long time with a mother raccoon.
She gave birth to three kittens.
He brought them to his broken home.
He became their father, he's got a family.

Out of blue

1

A little journey lasts like
the life of a star.
My backpack is full of
bullets and your agony.
You don't showcase your
love for the sunshine.
You want to see a pigeon
with a letter written in white
ink on its white feather.
We shoot toward the clouds
to kill the gloomy sky.
A Vulture falls down
all at once with blue blood.
Night comes and the sky dies.
We lose the only roof.

2

I keep the doors open.
You want more of hunting
sun with rosy air.
Out of blue when
a car stops on the street,
a man found inside the trunk
with an empty bottle of fuel.

You still want a rainbow
but others hate rain.
The driver goes away from
his anxiety and dives into water.
Another man found wrapped
around the wheel.
They are still alive among
the dead but they smell dead.
You still want a squirrel to talk
about your pain. Before I dig another
ocean to bury your wounds
you want me to shave your
hair so that you feel less heavy.
You still want the sun
but others bury the sunlight.
We keep the doors open for evils to
dwell in our body and eat the rest of us.

Ghost dinner

The other day in restaurant
I ordered the pizza to just
see if I have money in my
wallet. Waitress already
fell in love with me no one
ever knew about it. After
she served the table,
We had dinner together.
All half cooked leaves
I was eating like a goat.
She said she loved goats.
While checking out,
she demanded my heart
instead of money.
Her nails grew so fast.
My heart was on her palm.
Later she wore it on her finger.

Time travel

I thought I was in my twenties.
Although I already traveled
Another decade through time.
My mother says I am still a kid.
What I am actually no one knows.
Maybe when we were digging
The space, when time, for a second,
Rested upon the edge the firmament,
I was a digger, what I found was
A rusted egg of another universe.
I was healer, healed a galaxy from
The dying era. I was a traveler of space.
When my father left me in the ocean
Of scorn, I was a victim of violence.
My mother says I am still a kid.
What I am actually is a sufferer of
The summer that was supposed to be mild
On delicate skin instead burning it brutally.

Unexpected love

I forget your name and
the face that looked like water.
A park headed to heaven.
We found the way.
In a sloppy cascade,
unknown friend of mine
bathed after falling from hope.
She asked a towel
I gave her my long shirt.
We landed in empty heaven.
Years after on a half sunk boat
She looked at me like an eagle.
I did know who she was.
I could not swim her to the shore.
After she drowned, a girl
cried for a bad grade in math,
An angel that we borrowed from god.

A Green Earth

The other day the boy cried.
There was no water in the room.
A kid slept without dinner.
The breast of a woman was dried.
A blast of sunlight kissed the roof
after she walked alone into
the clouds and drove them away.
Birds hide gloom in the cherry.
There are rooms for everyone.
Rooms to burn sorrow and pain,
to plant more trees to give back
lost youth to our shabby home.
The lungs celebrate for clean air.
Waves of the ocean become tranquil.
The kid talks to the stars all night.

What is violence?

To a dormant glacier,
The reason to stay up is violence.

A wound there is the whole universe.

Acknowledgments

Climate Crisis in My Un(known) Dream and *Climate Injustice* first appeared in *Reckoning Press*.

About the Author

Lovely Raju is originally from Bangladesh, holds a BS in Applied Chemistry and Chemical Engineering from the University of Rajshahi. Seeking to nurture his poetic talents further, he pursued an MFA in creative writing from the University of Notre Dame. Lovely has worked as an assistant editor at Action Books, an international press for poetry and translations. His interests include ecopoetry, social justice poetry, and dream poetry. Nature and imagination are fundamental elements that weave through the fabric of his writing. Lovely incorporates various techniques to foster empathy and spread peaceful words through poetry. His debut full-length poetry book, HOPE, is out now from the Finishing Line Press. You can find him on Instagram @ppp_lovely_raju

FLOWERSONG
PRESS

FlowerSong Press nurtures essential verse
from, about, and throughout the borderlands.
Literary. Lyrical. Boundless.

Sign up for announcements about
new and upcoming titles at:

www.flowersongpress.com